I AM RIPTIDE

BY RIPTIDE'S MOMMA   A.K.A.   ROCHELLE LENTSCHKE

Rochelle

SPECIAL THANKS TO THE AMAZING TEAM THAT MADE MY VISION COME ALIVE.
I AM FOREVER GRATEFUL FOR THE PART THEY PLAYED:

JILL PETERSON   JILL IS MOST IMPORTANTLY, A DEAR FRIEND. SHE IS ALSO AN ACCOMPLISHED PHOTOGRAPHER,
AUTHOR, AND PUBLISHER AMONG HER MANY OTHER TALENTS AND GIFTS. HER PURSUIT OF HER
DREAM AND CALLING HAD RESIDUAL BLESSINGS ON MINE.
SOMETIMES YOU NEED A FRIEND WHO HAS BEEN WHERE YOU WANT TO GO.

JEFF HAZARD   JEFF HAS THE GIFT OF TAKING MY PHOTOGRAPHS AND TURNING THEM INTO MAGIC.
I'M SO GRATEFUL HE HAS SHARED HIS GIFTS AND TALENTS WITH ME.
SOMETIMES YOU NEED A FRIEND WHO CAN TAKE YOUR VISION AND GIVE IT WINGS.

LANA LENTSCHKE   LANA IS MY FAVORITE DAUGHTER. SHE HELPED ME FORM A STORY FROM MY JOURNAL AND
SHE ALSO LET ME LOVE HER DOG AS MUCH AS SHE DOES.
SOMETIMES YOU NEED A FRIEND WHO WILL LET YOU BORROW THEIR THINGS.

MELINDA CROW   MEL IS ALSO A GREAT FRIEND. AS AN ACCOMPLISHED AUTHOR, SHE UNDERSTOOD MY VISION
AND OFFERED GREAT SUGGESTIONS ALONG THE WAY.
SOMETIMES YOU NEED A FRIEND WHO IS WILLING TO TELL YOU THE TRUTH.

SYLVIE NUZZOLILO   SYLVIE IS THE OWNER OF TOP CLASS K9, LLC. IN CLEBURNE, TEXAS AND AN
ACCOMPLISHED TRAINER OF MULTIPLE DOGS. I LOVE HER SPIRIT AND AM FOREVER GRATEFUL
FOR THE PART SHE PLAYED IN OUR JOURNEY.
SOMETIMES YOU NEED A FRIEND WHO ISN'T AFRAID TO BOSS YOU AROUND WHEN NECESSARY.

RUBY WALSLEBEN   RUBY IS A DEAR FRIEND WHOSE SIMPLE DECISION TO COME VISIT ONE
DAY STARTED OUR JOURNEY AT THE NURSING HOME.
SOMETIMES YOU NEED A FRIEND WHO WILL MAKE THE TIME TO VISIT YOU EVEN WHEN IT ISN'T EASY.

LOIS HARFORD   ONE DAY LOIS SENT ME A SILLY LITTLE BOOK ABOUT A GUY AND HIS DOG.
I ENJOYED HIS BOOK AND I PRAY PEOPLE WILL ENJOY MINE.
SOMETIMES YOU NEED A FRIEND WHO HELPS YOU TAKE THE ROAD LESS TRAVELED.

COVER ART, ALL INCLUDED ARTWORK AND PHOTO EDITING BY J.L. HAZARD PET PORTRAITS.

* * * * * * * * *

WARDROBE CREDITS:
ALL VENDORS PROVIDE GREAT QUALITY, EXCELLENT CUSTOMER SERVICE AND REASONABLE PRICES:

LEATHER COLLARS ARE CUSTOM DESIGNS FROM ELLA'S LEAD AT WWW.ELLASLEAD.COM

FABRIC COLLARS ARE CUSTOM DESIGNS FROM COLLAR MANIA AT WWW.COLLARMANIA.COM

COATS/JAMMIES ARE CUSTOM MADE TO ORDER FROM MADE BY MEADOWCAT. PICTURES OF PRODUCTS AND ORDERING INFORMATION CAN BE FOUND ON THE FACEBOOK PAGE.

DOG TAGS ARE CUSTOM DESIGNS FROM AGGIES ANVIL. UNLIMITED OPTIONS ARE AVAILABLE. YOU CAN FIND THEM ON FACEBOOK.

Copyright © 2016

MANE & TALE PUBLISHING CO. + ROCHELLE LENTSCHKE

MANE AND TALE PUBLISHING CO.

PO BOX 115   IREDELL, TX 76649

IAMRIPTIDE2016@GMAIL.COM   254-230-3532

PROUDLY PRINTED IN THE USA BY TAYLOR PUBLISHING DALLAS, TEXAS

I am a Doberman

I am Riptide. A Riptide is a change of the current in the ocean. My family usually calls me Rip. My sister picked my name because she believed that I would

change the tide in our family and I would be different from other Dobermans. I am bigger and heavier than most. And I have silly ears. I can't see them, but people always ask about my ears. My mom says I grew so much bigger because my body had to make room for my Texas-sized heart.   I live with my family on a ranch in Texas. My family has a Dad, a Mom, a sister and a brother.

I'm 2 years old. I am not a puppy and I am not quite an adult. I am a "tween" and I am growing up and learning how to be a good dog. I'm finding out there is much to learn!

I am the first Doberman to live with my family. But I am not the only dog. I have two dog sisters. They are short, little dogs called Dachshunds. I love them. Their names are Pepper and Lola. Pepper is older and she doesn't like to play with me. I try to make her love me by giving her kisses but she doesn't want them.

Sometimes I want to kiss her so badly that I walk by and give her a kiss and then run away really fast. She doesn't like that either.

Lola is the same age as me and is my best friend. We have many fun adventures together.

I share all my toys and treats with Lola because she's my favorite. Sometimes she shares but sometimes she takes the treats under the bed. It makes me sad when she does because I can't fit under the bed. I could tell you lots of stories about Lola.

One time, I had a treat and she didn't because she had already eaten hers. I was saving mine. She wanted mine too, but I didn't want to share. While

we were inside the house, Lola barked like there was something scary outside. Because I protect my sisters, I dropped my treat and ran to the window to check it out. Lola grabbed my treat and tried to run away and hide it under the bed. My mom saw her and told her to leave it alone. I hurried back and picked up my treat.

A few minutes later, Lola barked again. Again, I dropped my treat and ran to the window. Lola grabbed my treat and started running down the hall. Mom told her to leave it alone again. I hurried back and picked it up again. When

Lola barked a third time, I took my treat with me! Mom laughed and told me she was proud of me. Lola cannot be trusted.

The thing I've learned about sisters is that some days they are tricky but most days they are nice.

We have lots of fun playing together. One of our favorite things to do together is to go rabbit hunting. When we hunt we get to use our noses and run as fast as we want. We have lots of rabbits on our ranch. We make a good team because Lola can smell the rabbits better than me but I can see over the tall grass. My favorite  thing to do is to run around as fast as I can through the tall grass and see if the rabbits run away. Lola likes to sniff her way through the grass and follow the rabbits instead.

When the rabbits run away, I run as fast as I can to chase them. Rabbits are tricky too. They run under fences and jump over things. I am too big to run under the fences, so Lola follows them under the fence and I go around. The problem with that plan is that Lola's legs are too short to run as fast as the

rabbits and when I go around, I never catch up fast enough. We have chased lots of rabbits, but we haven't caught any.

My mom is helping me learn to be a good dog by teaching me manners and good behavior commands. She also taught me some tricks. I can sit, lie down, shake with both paws, roll over, and give a high five. The hardest things are behavior commands like wait or stay because I like to go wherever my mom goes. She says that learning to obey all her commands will help keep me safe and make it easier to make new friends. I like to make friends with people and with other dogs.

I have taught them some cool things too. I taught them to make sure their words matched up with what they wanted me to do. All people should learn that. One time I got on my Mom's bed. My dad saw me and told me to get down. I obeyed his command and lay down on the bed. My mom laughed and told me to get off. Then I jumped off the bed. My mom says I am smart and I keep her on her toes. I don't know what that means. I like to make her laugh.

I have figured out that when I do silly things, it makes her laugh. And I do silly things. The whole family laughs at my sleeping positions. And sometimes I snore. My dad snores when he sleeps too.

My mom knows that I like to meet people and sometimes I get to go to work with her. Those days are fun! I have to ride in a car to get there and I like riding in her car. One day, I met a lady named Ruby who walked really slow and used a shiny silver thing to help her. My mom called it a walker. I could tell she was different than other ladies I had met, so I was careful with her. It made her happy. Ruby already knew how to scratch my back and that made me happy. Then we were all happy and it made my mom smile. I like to do things that make people smile.

I am a student

After my mom saw how gentle I was with Ruby, she wanted me to become a therapy dog. Therapy dogs are nice to special people who need gentle friends. We needed to learn how to behave around special friends like Ruby. My mom taught me all of the tricks and commands that I know. In order to become a therapy dog, we had more new things to learn. So, we had to go to school. One day we met someone called an Instructor because we had to take a test. Sometimes when you take a test, you need extra help from someone called an instructor. We got to take more rides in the car, so I was happy.

The instructor's name was Sylvie and she had a dog too! I was excited to meet her because I like to meet other dogs too. Her dog was different than me, she was smaller and her tail wagged when she saw us. Her name was Faith. Sylvie told us that she had adopted Faith from a shelter a long time ago.

Sylvie taught Faith all her good behavior commands and she knew more commands than me. Faith listened carefully to everything Sylvie told her and she did them all perfectly. We were impressed. Faith was friendly with my mom and me, we liked her. Faith and I wanted to play, but we had to go to school instead.

One of the things I needed to learn was how to meet people and dogs on a walk. Sylvie told me I could look at Faith and smile at her, but I had to sit and stay quietly by my mom. The first time we practiced, I couldn't help myself and I had to go say hello. The instructor told us to try again. The second time, I was still sitting but leaned as far as I could to kiss Faith. Sylvie said I must do it correctly. She told my mom that if I moved again, I would be in trouble. I knew what being in trouble meant because sometimes I get in trouble at home. The third time we practiced, the only thing I moved were my eyeballs. My mom and Sylvie laughed and she said I got extra credit points for my

listening skills. I think listening skills are a good thing to have when you are a student. I wanted to be a good dog like Faith because she was a star student. She had even won ribbons for her good behavior! Sylvie said that we also needed to learn to do all the things outside with lots of other people and dogs around.

The next time we went to school with Sylvie and Faith, we stopped for lunch. Mom and I usually had lunch outside in the park, but this was a new place. It was outside by a busy road. Mom said hearing the cars go by would give us good practice. I didn't mind the cars because we hear those at the park. But then I heard a noise I had never heard before and it was loud and scary! My mom said it was a train whistle. I wanted to jump in her lap, but she helped me be calm and wait for the noise to stop. I don't like trains and I'm glad there are no trains where we live. I was really happy to get back in the car and go see Faith and Sylvie. We practiced all our lessons outside in her yard. When we were almost done, the train whistle blew again. Mom and I both jumped. We didn't know the train went by Sylvie's house too. After our lesson, Sylvie said we were ready for the test and we all hoped the train whistle wouldn't blow that day.

When test day came, I didn't understand why my mom was nervous. I didn't know if she was afraid of the train or she didn't like tests. I had never taken a test before, but we had practiced and I knew that I would do what my mom told me. It was a windy day and there were lots of noises and things going on around us. I did everything exactly like they taught me and passed my test. I earned a ribbon just like the ones Faith had. Mom was proud of me. I like to make her proud. We earned a title called a Canine Good Citizen and it tells people that I listen to what my mom tells me to do and that I am polite and friendly with people and other dogs.

I am a Good Citizen

Because I am a good citizen, my mom said we needed to practice to become a therapy dog. And meeting new people was how we practiced. She started taking me to a place called a nursing home. There are lots of people that live there that are different from other people I had met. They live there because they need help from nurses. The nurses help them do things that their bodies cannot.

The first time we went, I met two ladies. My mom said we needed to show them that I had good manners and show them that I liked meeting people. They were nice. They told me I was handsome and that my ears were cute. I like when people tell me I am handsome! The next time we went, we sat outside and watched the people. There were lots of new smells and sounds at this place and my mom knew that I needed to learn about the place a little at a time. I met ladies that walked with their legs and ladies that rolled in a chair. I tried to meet a nurse, but she was afraid to come outside. I smiled at her, but she was still afraid. I don't understand why some people don't want to meet me. Each time I visited, I met more ladies. I want to share what I learned from them.

ANISA: What I learned from Anisa is that caring about people makes them feel valued. Anisa was my first friend at the home. I met her on our first visit. She is the lady that helps me make friends and shows us around. My mom says she's the boss. I don't know what that means, but I think she's kind of like the mom of the place. She tells everyone when we are coming to visit and introduces us to people that aren't able to come to see us. We follow her to their rooms and she tells us their names.

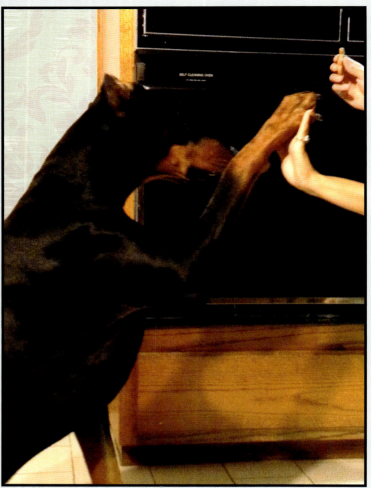

I like Anisa. My mom likes her too. We like her because she was the first one to believe in us and she is always happy to see us. Sometimes you need a friend who's willing to believe in you when you are young and trying to grow up.

BEVERLY: What I learned from Beverly is that sometimes words don't matter as much as people think. She was one of the first residents I met. She sits in a chair that rolls. She moves differently than some of the other people and her words sound different than the ones I hear at home. I had not seen anyone like her before. I watched her closely and listened to the sounds she was making. I walked over to her to see if she wanted to be my friend. I didn't understand her sounds. But when I looked into her eyes, I could see that her heart was kind and friendly. I wanted to make it easy for her to be my friend, so I put my head in her lap. She started to giggle and she patted my head many times. Her pats were much harder than how my family pats my head, but I liked it just the same.

The next few times I saw Beverly, her words were easier to understand and she even said my name! It was the first word she said that we understood. Now, her hands move softly when she pats me. My mom said I helped her by giving her something soft to touch. One time my mom and I showed her my high five trick and it made her smile. The next time we saw her, she kept saying "high five" over and over. My mom said we made her happy.

Sometimes you find out that what is in people's hearts is more important than the words say with their mouths.

MARGARET: What I learned from Margaret is that being friendly is a good thing. I met Margaret on the first day we visited the home. She also sits in a chair, but she can roll it all by herself. She has lots of friends and talks more than the other ladies.

The first day I met her, she told me stories about her dogs. She once owned little dogs like Lola the Dachshund. Margaret likes to tell me stories. She was the first person to understand that even though I look big and scary, that I'm not scary at all. I am friendly just like her. Margaret comes to talk with me every time I visit. When I first started going inside with the people, some were unsure if I was friendly. Margaret would tell them that I was a good boy. One time I heard her yell "I'm coming Riptide!" as she rolled her chair as fast as she could toward me. It was nice to feel welcome.

I think she likes my name because she says it louder than all the other people do. She says my whole name like Mommas do when you are in trouble. But I know that I am not in trouble with Margaret. She is my biggest fan and she likes it when my mom takes pictures of us together. Taking pictures makes my mom happy, she does it all the time.

I'm glad Margaret is my friend. Sometimes you need a friend who helps you meet new people when you look different than other dogs.

MAXINE: What I learned from Maxine is that dressing nicely sometimes helps you feel better. Maxine didn't like me at first and she wouldn't get very close. She did like to look at me and tell me that she liked my necklaces. My mom calls them collars and they are how I dress nicely. The more I visited, the more she wanted to talk to me. Maxine is different from the other ladies I met because she doesn't sit in a chair, she walks with her legs. She has black, shiny hair like mine. She always dresses nicely and uses big words when she talks like my sister. I think she likes to talk to my mom more than me, but I don't mind.

One day when we visited, she was the first one to come see me. I stood closer to her than usual so she would know that I cared but I didn't get too close. She told me she was sad. I already knew, but I listened anyway. She told me that when I came all dressed up in my collar and bowtie, she wasn't sad anymore.

I thought bowties only made my mom happy. We brought her a card with my picture on it and she told us about how my pictures make her giggle. It's good that my mom takes lots of pictures of me because I like to help Maxine find her giggle. She told me she had been sick for a long time but I didn't notice. Dogs only care about what's on the inside of people. Sometimes you can look good on the outside and not feel very good on the inside.

WESLEY: What I learned from Wesley is that affection is important. Wesley usually stays in his room when we visit. Or he watches T.V. in a room with a friend that doesn't get out of bed. Wesley has a chair that rolls but he needs help rolling it because his hands work differently than some people. I have visited him a couple of times in his room and he is always happy to see me.

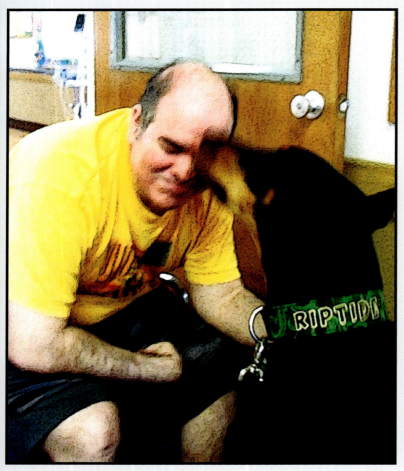

He likes to rub my back and I like it too!

One time when we visited, a nurse brought him to see me in the lobby. I was so excited to see him that I walked right to him and let him pet me. My mom taught me to stand in front of his chair so that he can easily reach and pet me because petting me makes him smile. My mom asked if he wanted a picture with me and he did. My mom always makes me sit for pictures, so I sat down next to him. Right before my mom snapped the picture, Wesley leaned closer to me. I thought it was be-cause he wanted a kiss and so I gave him three or four!

My mom was worried that we would get into trouble. A little while later, we heard him telling Anisa about getting kisses and he was laughing. Then my mom knew we weren't in trouble and she felt better. She should learn to trust me more. She can only see their faces but I can see their hearts. Sometimes you just have to let your heart lead the way even if you give sloppy kisses.

ROBERT: What I learned from Robert is that sometimes it's hard to change how people think. He sits in a chair that he can roll by himself. He likes to talk to my mom. He told her that his initials were R.I.P. and he thought it was funny that his name was the same as mine.

He also told her a story about his Weimeraner dog he had when he was young. Weimeraners are big dogs too. He told her that his dog was protective of their family and told us about a time his dog protected his little sister from a stranger. He said that I would probably protect my family too. He was right because I look out for my little dog sisters on all our adventures. He talked for a long time. I got tired and lie down by my mom so she could listen. After he finished his story, he asked what kind of dog I was. My mom told him I was a Doberman Pinscher and he said, "Dobermans are mean!" I was still lying down listening to them and my mom said, "Does that look like a mean dog to you?" I smiled at him but he didn't smile back.

 It was a long time before I saw Robert again. The next time I saw him, he was smiling at me and he thanked my mom for bringing me to visit. Sometimes it takes a long time to change how people think.

The gentlemen I meet do not talk as much as the ladies. They watch T.V. more than talk. They like to tell me about how big I am and that I am the biggest dog they have ever seen. I think I'm the only big dog that comes to visit.

When we started visiting the nursing home, we found out that I am just the right size for these people. My mom says that it is a good thing that I am big because the people don't have to bend over very far to pet me. It's easy to reach me when they stand up and when they sit in a chair. And when they can't get out of bed, I am just the right height for that too. My mom says that I am perfectly designed for the work I am doing. It's fun to me because I love to help people feel happy and see their smiles.

We met several other people. We met some that didn't talk at all. Some that didn't sit in a chair or use a stick to walk. Some were older and

some were younger. Some were friendly and some were not. Some liked meeting me and some were frightened or not interested in me at all. There is something to be learned from the ones that like us as well as from the ones that don't. Sometimes when people don't like us, it is usually about them and not about us.

All the people I met are different and they are all special to me on my journey of learning what makes ME special. Even though we are all made differently, we each have special gifts and talents. Do you know what it is that makes YOU special? If not, you should learn.

I am colorful

My mom likes to dress me in fancy clothes. And one day I wore lots of things. My mom dressed me like a rock star named Elvis. She says I am a rock star too. Dressing me like that made her laugh and she said it would make my friends at the nursing home laugh too.

One day when we visited, she dressed me in a fancy collar, cape, jewelry, and a wig with glasses. She said this was how an Elvis dog would look. She said we were going to visit our friends at the nursing home and we would take treats to them. When we got there, all the people were laughing and smiling at me. Most of them wanted to pet me and some of them wanted a picture with me. My mom was right; they did like my Elvis suit! I wasn't sure I liked it because parts of it kept falling off.

All of our favorite friends were there and we even got to meet more people. They liked the treats we brought for them. I understand because I get happy when people give me treats too.

Another time when we visited, Mom made me wear a special coat. It was cold, so I was glad I had a coat. She said it made me look like Santa Claus. I don't know him. But Mom said that my friends would be happy to see me in my coat. We took more treats for them and they were happy again.

This time I got to see all of the people and my sister came along too! It was fun to meet each one and give them a treat. We went to lots of rooms and every person had a smile that day. They even had a plastic man that had a coat like mine.

We go visit our friends every month. Sometimes I wear collars. Sometimes I wear collars and ties and I wear coats when I am cold. My mom likes for me to dress nicely. My mom says gentlemen should always dress nicely when they go visit friends. I didn't know I was a gentleman, I thought I was a Doberman.

She must be right because they always tell me I look handsome. Even the nurses want to take my picture sometimes. Moms know lots of cool things. I'm glad mine helps me make new friends.